FORGIVE ME, SUCCESS:

Life Guide 101

DARIUS BROWN

FORGIVE ME, SUCCESS: LIFE GUIDE 101

by
Darius L. Brown

* * * * *

PUBLISHED BY:
Darius L. Brown

ISBN: 0578077892
ISBN-13: 9780578077895

CONTENTS

INTRODUCTION

"If you are not pursuing your purpose in life, you are living a fancy death."

Every day I see many people commuting from place to place to get something accomplished. As I observe their actions, I ask myself, "Where are they going so fast? Why are they doing what they are doing?" Everyone wants to be successful in life, but we have missed the mark in understanding what success really is. Success is not a happening or an event; it is a series of intended outcomes coming to pass. In all reality, success is not the final desired goal of life, but rather it is fulfillment. Anything that does not lead to your personal fulfillment is not success. It has become a misconceived concept about vast materialism. Sadly, this is far from the truth. Success is the product of three foundational principles: the identification of purpose, vision, and the fulfillment of action.

THE PRINCIPLES OF SUCCESS

Purpose

To everything, there is a why. Therefore, your life has a purpose and you must find out why you're on earth.

Vision

After you discover why you're here, the only way to express who you are to the world is through developing a unique vision for your life.

Action

The possession of this awesome vision requires work. You have to put action behind your vision.

Fulfillment

Fulfillment is the result of your purpose being perfectly manifested andrevealed to the world.

I have personally practiced and experienced the principles in this book, and I want you to live the fulfilled life you deserve, and produce success on a daily basis. Come on a journey with me as I help you to strategically discover your purpose, develop a vision, and take action towards the life You were born to **live**!

PART I

DISCOVERING YOUR PURPOSE

"If you aren't pursuing your purpose in life, you're simply living a fancy death."

CHAPTER I
UNDERSTANDING YOURSELF AND OTHERS

THE BEGINNING OF LIFE

WHO AM I!? WHERE DO I GO!? WHAT CAN I DO!?

These three questions resonate unconsciously in the hearts of every human being on earth. All 6.9 billion people on earth are burdened with responsibility of discovering who they are, why they are, and what they can offer to the world. If you are on this earth, you were put here by the Creator because of a need that has to be met. You are not a mistake, but a product of purpose. The mystery of purpose discovery is a struggle for the majority of the world's population on earth. Most education and religious systems deviate away from this pertinent topic. Furthermore, most people do not understand that purpose discovery mainly comes by identifying the unique gifts you have been endowed with since birth. Fortunately, your purpose is easier to find than you think. Let's take an odyssey into the matter of gift discovery.

INDENTIFYING PURPOSE THROUGH YOUR GIFTS

In order to understand how to impact the people with your specific gift, you must understand the way the Creator designed man.

THE DESIGN OF MAN

Man is designed in the Image of the Creator, 3 in 1.

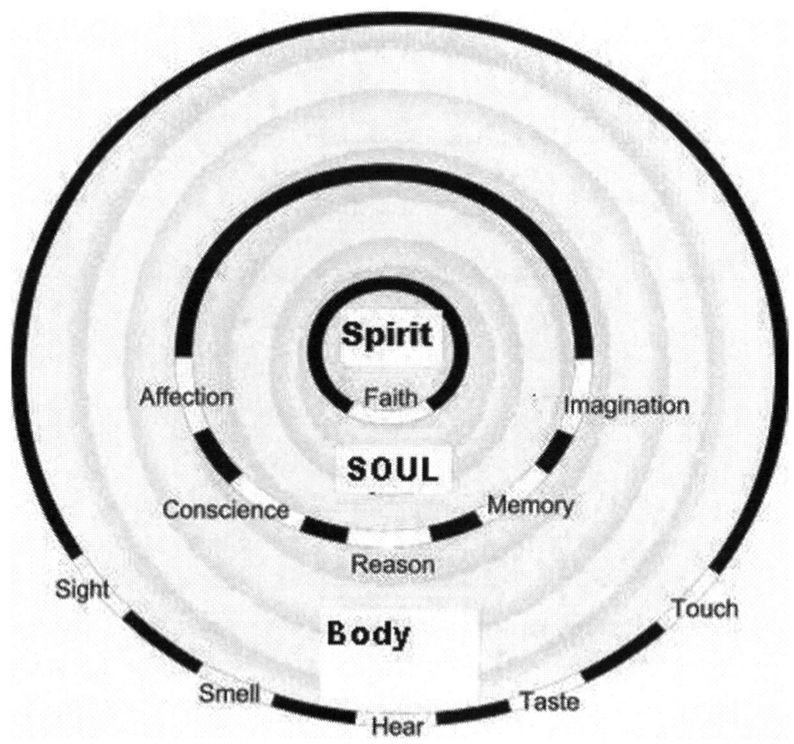

THE COMPOSITION OF MAN:

<u>Spirit:</u> The Spirit in you represents your motivation, attitude, and the intentions behind your passion and purpose for living.

Let's talk about the soul. We need to understand the design of the soul completely.

<u>Imagination</u>: image: a mental representation; idea; conception. (2) A creative ability B: ability to confront and deal with a problem.

Image-Nation *(a nation of images that work together to acquire something desired or to solve a problem.) – Darius Brown*

Conscience: (1) Intentions or character together with a feeling of obligation to do right or be good.

Memory: (1) the time within which past events can be or are remembered.

Reasoning:
(1) The thing that makes some fact intelligible.
(2) The power of comprehending, inferring, or thinking, especially in orderly, rational ways.

Affections:
(1) A moderate feeling or emotion.
(2) A tender feeling toward another; fondness.

Our souls are the core of who we are and we must understand that our gifts penetrate other people souls which causes them to react in gratitude and also to monetarily respond and pay to benefit from your gift.

INTRODUCTION OF THE FLESH

Flesh: The flesh is nothing more than excellently structured dirt and water. The Flesh is what makes us (soul) able to operate on earth. Without it, we would not exist on earth. We possess a flesh to live out our purpose on earth and enjoy the gifts and privileges the Creator put us here to partake of. Every gift that is given from the Creator to human beings is designed to impact the souls of people. There are only 5 possible ways to impact the soul. Every business industry or religious institution in the world is based off of these 5 windows that impact the soul.

THE 5 GATEWAYS TO THE SOUL

The soul is impacted by these 5 Gates of The Flesh:

- **Sight**: (1) A thing regarded as worth seeing
  (2) The act of looking at or beholding
- **Hearing:** the ability to perceive sound
- **Taste:** the ability to detect the flavor of substances such as food, certain minerals, and poisons, etc.
- **Touch:** to bring a bodily part into contact with especially so as to perceive through the tactile sense
- **Smell:** to detect or become aware of as if by the sense of smell

*All 5 of these gates directly impact the soul which is our imagination, conscience, memory, reasoning and affections.

CHAPTER II
FINDING YOUR GIFTS

Every business and every institution that has ever been established has catered to these 5 gateways because it is the only way people can be impacted. Therefore, your gift lies within any of these areas. Your gift is something that you are passionate about doing, and also something that you can do well that makes someone say "I like this" or "I love this." Your gift is something that you do from your heart that you may feel is needed and can benefit others.

For Example, I think about athletes like Michael Jordan who had a special way of impacting billions of souls through his ability to play the game of basketball well and letting you "see" his gift being put to work. He impacted souls through acknowledging his ability to make people see the gift of athleticism. He persuaded people to buy his products and was featured in many commercials because of his gifts in making people see something

Musical artists like Tupac Shakur, who left a mark on the world with his gift in making you "hear" something. He would read books, write songs and record them to make you hear something that would move your soul. Everyone has to eat to survive, and different cultures have their preferences. Kernel Sanders, who had the gift of cooking, started Kentucky Fried Chicken, better known as KFC in 1952. He used his gift to create a product that will live on for generations and impact billions of people through the gateway of taste. When you're hungry and you pass by a KFC, your imagination starts thinking about the chicken and products KFC serves. When you smell the chicken cooking you can almost taste it. You're connected with them for life because he used his gift to impact your soul.

When I think of scented fragrances and air fresheners, I think about several people who have perfumes and colognes. SC Johnson Family Company who created Glades air freshener has made products that have been influencing billions of souls worldwide through the gateway of smelling.

Have you ever smelled something and said to someone, "This reminds me of something or someone?" You can see clearly that the gateway of smell impacts the soul's memory. When your body feels hot while you are inside your house, car or maybe even at work, what is the first thought that comes to your head? Most likely it will be to turn on the air conditioner to make your body cooler. You see, someone had to use their gift in creativity of science to figure out how to make a product that can alter the present conditions of an atmosphere's temperature to make your body comfortable at all times. If Willis Havilland never exercised his engineering gifts to create this marvelous invention, air conditioning in 1902, we would have some very uncomfortable living conditions.

Therefore, his gift impacted our souls in every way by making our bodies "feel" good.

Through these examples, I urge you to look into your soul and ask yourself "What is it that I can do or what can I offer to impact somebody's soul through sight, taste, smell, touch or hearing?"

PART 1 - PRINCIPLES AND KEYS (DISCOVERING YOUR PURPOSE AND FINDING YOU GIFTS)

1. Understanding your purpose is the beginning of true life.

2. Your purpose is directly connected to your gift.

3. You can only discover your purpose by identifying your gifts (Some people may have more than one prominent gift)

4. A gift is something given voluntarily without payment in return, as to show favor toward someone, or to honor an occasion. (2) A special ability or capacity; natural endowment.

5. The purpose of a gift is for it to be given to its rightful recipient.

6. You were given a gift from the Creator to give to the world.

7. Your gifting is what gives you value.

8. Your gifting preserves your life.

9. When you discover your gift, you are not wanted but *needed* by the world.

10. Your gift was given to you to impact someone else's life.

11. In order to find your gift and impact the world, you must understand what you are gifted in.

12. To acknowledge where your gifts lie, you must know how humans are influenced and affected by exterior forces.

PART II

DEVELOPING THE VISION

"Vision is the headlights to the vehicle called purpose which drives you towards your destiny."
– Darius Brown

INTRODUCTION OF VISION

"A vision is not a vision if it does not enhance the lives of others spiritually, mentally, or physically."

There is something that all humans need to find. It is the most essential discovery in life. It is more valuable than finding gold, silver, platinum, diamonds or vast amounts of crude oil. It is a vehicle that is fully equipped and able to take you towards your predetermined destiny. In the passenger seat, there is something called "Success" and the gas tank is filled up with motivation to bring glory to the Creator of this vehicle because the Creator knows exactly why this vehicle was created and what it can do. This is the most important discovery in life to every individual. This vehicle that can take you toward your destiny is called "purpose."

Furthermore, purpose is the greatest discovery in life, but it is the first and foundational step towards your destiny. Purpose is the fully equipped vehicle that is ready to go and waiting for you to get in.

So you get in this vehicle called purpose and you're ready to go. Yet you still see things on the outside that have not changed once after you have entered the vehicle. Things still seem a little dark and unclear when you look with your physical eyes. In order for you to start driving towards your destiny, you have to visualize where you want to go. This vehicle of purpose has a control in it called "vision." Now vision is like the headlights on a car. When it is dark outside and your natural eyes can't see where to go, the headlights give you the ability to see where you are going to reach your destination.

Though things still seem dark and uncertain after you discover your purpose and gifts, vision gives you the power to see where you are going in life.

CHAPTER III
THE DIRECTION DEVELOPING A VISION PLAN

"The only thing worse than being blind is
having sight but no vision"
– **Helen Keller**

September 11, 2001, a catastrophic event took place that shocked the world and is still affecting the lives of many people today. There were two buildings in Lower Manhattan that were a part of the World Trade Center, known as the "Twin Towers". They were destroyed by a "terrorist group" that flew two aircrafts into each building. Nearly three thousand people were killed in this incident leaving many families in shambles. These buildings were so massive and monumental, that people came from all over the world to visit. I am a Jersey City, New Jersey native myself, and in Jersey City, you could go to several locations in the city and look up and see the Twin Towers. I lived in a different city, but the colossal size of these buildings which were one hundred and ten stories each, were noticed prominently.

The proposal to build the Twin Towers was initially made in 1946. However, the building process did not start until 1962 due to legal and tax issues. When the time came to start building in 1962, an architect named Minoru Yamasaki was chosen to be the lead architect for the two buildings. The buildings were not constructed until 1965. The completion of the North Tower was December 23, 1970 and the South Tower was July 19, 1971.

WRITE THE VISION AND MAKE IT PLAIN

The time span between the initial concept of building the Twin Towers and its completion, from 1946-1971, is twenty five years. This implies that when you are about to do something great with your life, your vision has to be developed, tested for authenticity and be approved. In 1962 the building process of the Twin Towers started, but the construction did not start. The building process always begins with a plan and a vision. When lead architect Minoru Yamasaki was selected to start the building process, he had the responsibility of finishing the Twin Towers before construction even began.

Vision does not start when physical things appear, vision causes physical things to appear and happen. Minoru Yamasaki designed and finished the Twin Towers on paper and then the construction started in 1965 which is 3 years after the building process started. The time in between 1962 and 1965 is where the vision was made plain and written down. All the office spaces, elevators, bathrooms etc were completed before a piece of steel was even placed to the foundation. Vision operates as the desired ending of a thing before it is physically established.

My question to you is "What is the 'Twin Tower' in your heart that you may want to build?" The innate gifts you have and the passion to benefit the lives of others has to be visualized into reality. You have to write your vision down on paper, or type it up like Minoru Yamasaki did before the Twin Towers were built. Ask yourself, where can I see myself in the next year, five years or ten years? You cannot move in your life's purpose if you do not know where you want to go. When you write your vision down, do not think about any physical limitations that you may face.

Some of you may not have a job, or you've lost your job and feel that all hope is gone. However, you have not lost your skills, talents and gifts. This can be the best time to turn on the vision in your life because the pressure is on. What you have to do now is make your skills, gifts and passions available for the world to acknowledge what you supply. Now you can take the lid off how much you're truly worth. You do not deserve hourly pay; you deserve valued payment. This is your chance to activate the vision in your heart, to see how you can impact the world with the gifts you possess.

When I stopped working my last job in April of 2009, I had a dream in my heart that I would not work a job another day in my life. I finally understood that if someone can hire me and to be a CEO, why can't I be a CEO? I worked as a cashier in a bowling in South Florida, and I was very good at giving great customer service. While at home, I was sleeping on the floor in my little brother's room because there were thirteen people living in a three bedroom apartment. With no purpose and vision for my life, the only thing I could pursue to make this situation easier was money. So I requested to work more hours, which my manger approved because I was a great employee. I started working six days a week almost fifty hours a week. As I pursued money and more hours, something still felt like it was missing. I would work and get paid $9.00 per hour yet at the end of some of my shifts, the cash register would total to thousands of dollars. Then, I knew something was wrong. While I was make $9.00 per hour and "chasing Friday" to meet immediate bills, the visionaries who started the bowling alley company was making thousands of dollars a day. I was employed by someone else's vision beside mine. They discovered their passion and developed a vision of how to make their gifts available for others to appreciate. You can do the same thing too. No one on this earth can share your gift the way you do. It is your responsibility to present your gifts to the world by developing a vision to impact the world with the dreams in your heart.

Do not think about resource limitations when you write down the dream in your heart that you would like to see become a reality. The Creator has given you limitless potential to bring the gifts in your heart out to the physical world in a way never seen before. By writing down the vision and establishing the things you would like to do in your life time, you open the door for opportunities and resources to come to you. When you understand your vision and live by it, it protects you from chasing money. Money is a miserable thing to chase because you can never have enough. You would do anything to get it when that is all you are chasing. Money is a lousy commodity to be pursued. You should desire the fulfillment of life through the purpose the Creator has predestined for you. Money and resources are attracted to the vision you write down and live out. When your vision is established, you would know exactly where to spend the money when you receive it.

PART 2 - PRINCIPLES AND KEYS (DEVELOPING YOUR VISION)

1. Vision is seeing your purpose with a clear mental image.

2. Vision is seeing your future in the present.

3. Vision is the direction to your predestined destiny.

4. The gift that you have in your heart is connected to your purpose and has to be visualized into reality.

5. You cannot move in your purpose in life if you do not know where you want to go.

6. By writing down your vision and establishing the things you would like to do in your lifetime, you open the door for opportunities and resources to come to you.

PART III

TAKING ACTION

"Activating your vision is like turning on the headlights of your life"

CHAPTER IV
AGGRESSIVELY ADVANCING

THE ATTITUDE OF VISION

When we approach any decision making situation in life, it always begins with a motivation. The motivation behind what you're doing creates the attitude and driving force behind your decision. When taking action towards living a successful life, it starts with writing down the vision and making it plain and simple. Before you write your vision down, you must not only discover your unique gifts but understand the attitude behind VISION. Vision itself has an attitude to defy the circumstances of what is seen and to bring the unseen to the physical realm. Vision has components that must be appreciated before writing down any goals and plans. The biggest principle to writing down a dynamic vision for your life is to not LIMIT YOURSELF. As we approach this final step to being successful, you must remember these simple components about vision.

WHEN WRITING YOUR VISION DOWN, REMEMBER THESE PRINCIPLES:

There are no physical limitations
There are no financial limitations
There are no educational limitations
Last but not least,
THERE ARE NO LIMITATIONS TO THE POTENTIAL THAT LIES WITHIN YOU!!!!

HOW TO TAKE ACTION

Taking action requires a plan. A plan requires a gift, and a gift requires motivation. As we discussed earlier, you must write down the vision before you act. Writing down the vision is the first part of action, but it can also be the most intimidating part. Most people do not want to encounter who they can potentially be. The responsibility to respond to our destiny can seem to be heavy. However responding to your destiny is non-negotiable. Writing down the vision is the foundation of a productive and fulfilling life. As we conclude, I would like to help you take immediate action by guiding you through my personal process of writing down my vision plan for one year.

THE "GIFTED VISIONARY WORKSHOP"

(WORKSHOP IS ATTACHED AT THE END OF THE BOOK)

The "Gifted Visionary Workshop," consists of a 4 step process which is necessary for immediate action towards your destiny.

The first step in writing down my gifted visionary plan is composing a ***Vision map.***

STEPS TO DRAWING A VISION MAP

**This step is important is because it has scientifically been proven that the brain recognizes and remembers shapes and colors more than any straight line college rule paper document. Whatever you desire in your life, you can use the process to achieve it to define a clear guiding vision for your life.*

When conducting a vision map you want to first get a blank display board or just a blank piece of paper. On the blank board or paper, you can draw a circle in the middle and then put your name and also a nickname for yourself pertaining to who you are and what you plan to succeed in.

After you draw the circle in the middle of the paper, you are to draw four curvy lines coming from the circle.

These four curvy lines represent a specific gift you may have or something you love to. On these lines think about what you love to do and put it in one word. For example, if you love a certain type of music, put the word music down on the branch.

After you write the word down on the branch, make small stems to the branch concerning specifics of what you would like to do with your gift. For example, if you have music on the branch, on each stem you may want to describe what style of music; hip hop, southern or northern, motivational etc. For every branch that you write down a gift for, you will follow this procedure.

You may want to also add color to your map as well.

2. Writing down Vision Plans and Goals

The second step is simple but essential. For me this is the longest part because it requires the ***"attitude of vision"*** to be active as mentioned earlier. You have to sit somewhere solitarily until you have written down all the desires of where you would like to see yourself by using your gift. For beginners, you may want to write no more than a one and a half page to avoid feeling discouraged when you look at all the goals. However, by all means if you desire to write more, be prepared to plan longer than a one - year plan.

3. Giving Deadlines to Your Vision

When you give deadlines to your vision, you are calling forth action to preside immediately. You may plan your vision for several years to come, or even for the rest of your life. Although plans are subject to change, you still have a plan to be changed. Without deadlines, you will never move into your life of fulfilled desires. Originally, I started out with writing down a one - year plan, but now I have a twenty year plan written down and soon a fifty year plan. So I ask that you start with writing a one - year plan.

First you must add your goals and objectives from the previous step and plug them into your one - year vision plan. The most important factor about this step is to break your year down in quarters. When doing this step, you want to organize your goals in sequence depending on which ones are more likely to occur first.

- ***Jan-March***
- ***April-June***
- ***July-September***
- ***October-December***

4. Writing down a daily to - do list

Writing out a daily to - do list urges you to take action everyday by writing down plans to work toward the goals of your one - year vision plan. Every day, you should be working towards being successful and experiencing fulfillment. It is very important to write your to - do list for the next day, each evening. Once you write the to - do list the night before, your mind will have it programmed to fulfill what you planned for the next day, and even in your sleep your brain will still be working to bring your daily goals to pass. Also, put times next to your goals and have an estimated time for your goals to be met throughout the day. Waste no time and be diligent in pursuing your plans!

CONCLUSION

Now that we have addressed the components of success and how to live a fulfilled life, I implore you to take action and live a progressive life. You are the key to your success. There is no other way to achieve your desired goal in life, unless you understand the principles in this book. Your success is as big as your vision. Your vision is catapulted from identifying your unique gifts and those gifts are connected to your purpose. You must take action on your vision and manifest your purpose to the world. To conclude, I would like to leave you with a few of my quotes to remember:

FORGIVE ME, SUCCESS PRINCIPLES

- **"Success is a product of three foundational principles." The identification of purpose, vision and action that must be applied."**

- **"You are not a mistake, but a product of purpose."**

- **"Vision itself has an attitude to defy the circumstances of what is seen and to bring the unseen to the physical realm."**

- "Vision operates as the desired ending of a thing before it is physically established."
- "Activating your vision is like turning on the headlights of your life."
- "Success is only measured by how you live out your purpose."
- "When you are pursuing your destiny, you cannot let "tired" make you tired, you tell "tired" when you're tired."
- "Success is the trail of someone relentlessly pursuing their purpose and destiny."
- "If you don't constantly change, the pain of staying the same will kill you!"
- "True vision is tested. True vision is tempted. But it lasts even after the storm. Are you still living the vision out, after the storm?"
- "Winners believe in their dreams when that is all they have!!!" - BELIEVE!"
- "Being successful and constantly improving in all you do is simple: Plan, Do and Review. But have a vision of reviewing what you did before you do it."
- "Some people take time to plan a vacation trip, but never sit down and spend time writing down plans for their life. No vision, no life."
- "Success is a thin line between making a living and living life by the vision in your heart."

- **"Show us something the world has never seen, you were born to do so."**
- **"Vision is the oxygen of the spirit."**
- **"There is no such thing as a weakness. It is only an area of improvement. ELIMINATE EXCUSES!"**

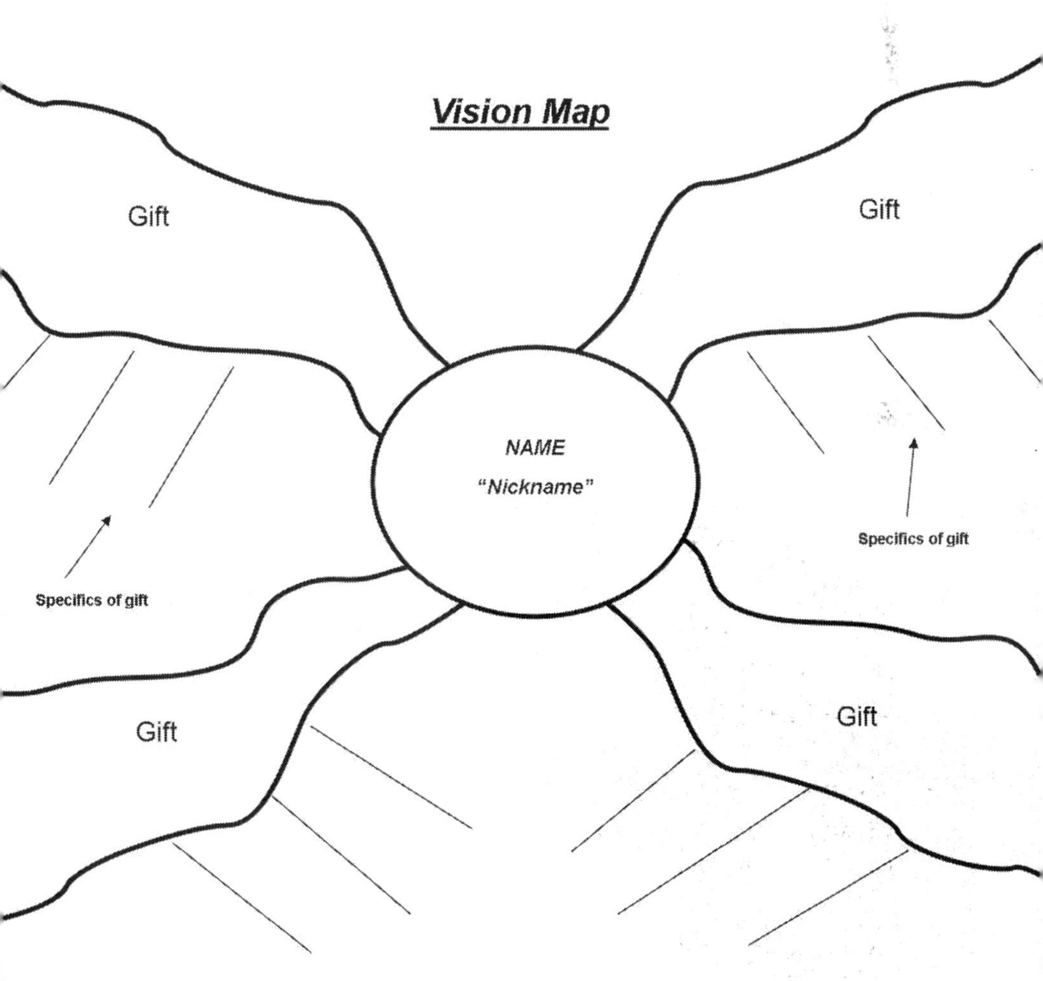

GOALS AND OBJECTIVES

1 YEAR VISION PLAN

JANUARY – MARCH

APRIL – JUNE

JULY – SEPTEMBER

OCTOBER – DECEMBER

WEEKLY SCHEDULE

____
(Your Name)

FOR THE WEEK OF ______________________________

Monday

Tuesday

Wednesday

Thursday

Friday

Saturday

Sunday

NOTES

TO DO:

CALLS TO MAKE

SPECIAL THANKS

First and foremost, I would like to thank God for giving me the courage and peace to produce this project throughout all circumstances. This could have not been possible without supernatural help and support. I also want to thank those who supported me through the tough time I was going through when I first started writing this book. You know who you are, and I would not be where I am if it weren't for your prayers, encouragement, phone calls, and emails. I want thank my mom, Iris Hannah-Brown and brothers, Torrell, Cortland, Marcus and Antoine who supported and pushed me to do what seemed impossible or unreasonable for someone coming from our background. I love you guys! Also, I want to thank Dr. Myles Munroe, Nathaniel Patterson, Raymond Eneas, and Corey and Angela Poole for depositing the seeds in my life to be the man I am today. Special thanks to the entire Employed By My Vision, Inc. team (Jessica Señorin, Omar Tolbert, Joshua Jean, and Nevetta Barton) who tremendously built me up and never let me become doubtful. There are no words to express how much I love you. To my friend Peta-Gaye Nelson, who took her careful time to edit this project, I love you, my sister, and I thank you. I also want to thank my past, present, and future for inspiring me to excel in every area of my life.

BRING DARIUS BROWN OF EMPLOYED BY MY VISION INC. TO YOUR NEXT EVENT. CHECK OUT OUR SERVICES AT THE CONTACT INFO BELOW.

Contact:
Darius Brown
CEO/Founder
Employed By My Vision Inc.
www.employedbymyvision.com
Email: info@employedbymyvision.com
Facebook: Employed By My Vision Inc.
Twitter: @dariusviceroy

ABOUT THE AUTHOR

From Darius' Perspective:

"When I stopped working my last job in April of 2009, I had a dream in my heart that I would not work a job another day in my life. I finally understood that if someone can hire me and be a CEO, why can't i be a CEO? I worked as a cashier in a bowling alley in South Florida, and I was very good at giving great customer service. While at home, I was sleeping on the floor in my little brother's room because there were 13 people living in a 3 bedroom apartment. With no purpose discovery and vision for my life, the only thing I could pursue to make this situation easier was money. So I requested to work more hours, which my manager approved because I was a great employee. I started working 6 days a week almost 50 hrs a week. As I pursued money and more hours, something still felt like it was missing. I would work and get paid $9 per hour yet at the end of some of my shifts, my cash register would total to thousands of dollars. Then, I knew something was wrong. While I make $9 an hour chasing money to meet immediate bills, the visionaries who started the bowling alley company was making thousands of dollars a day. The point is, I was employed by other people's vision, people who discovered their passion and developed a vision on how to make their gifts transferable for others to appreciate. You too can do the same thing because no one on this earth share your gift the way you do, and it is your responsibility to present your gifts to the world by developing a vision to impact the world with the dreams in your heart.

My life experiences have influenced my motivational speaking career. In the roughest part of northern New Jersey, Jersey City, I was raised by a single mother of five boys. When I was 10 years old, I was relocated to Miami, Florida with my family. After moving to South Florida, family and I experienced major financial hardships, being homeless and living with others for years until my family and I our own place to call home. I express these experiences through my speaking engagements to inspire and encourage others to know that despite anything, we can still be victorious in life."

Darius's expertise in the field of purpose discovery, vision development & empowerment has been sought after by many organizations and institutions including:

- *Tully's House Detention Center – Newark, NJ*
- *Christ The Rock International – Brooklyn, NY*
- *Rutgers University- Newark Campus*
- *Broward College – Davie, Fl*
- *University of Miami*
- *Florida International University*
- *Highland Avenue Church of Jamaica, NY*
- *Higher Call World Outreach Church – Pittsburgh, PA*
- *Florida Bible Christian School*
- *Dade Christian School*
- *Covenant House – Newark, NJ*
- *Second Baptist Church – Baldwin, NY*
- *The Y.E.S Center – Newark, NJ*
- *Faith Fellowship Ministries – Sayreville, NJ*
- *Youth Advocate Program – New Brunswick, NJ*
- ***And many more ....***

OTHER PRODUCTS AND SERVICES

INSPIRATIONAL MUSIC by Darius Brown aka ViceRoy

The Shift EP: REVELATION –
www.cdbaby.com/viceroy33 or on iTunes

Made in the USA
San Bernardino, CA
10 January 2017